Nude Siren

Nude Siren

Poems by
Peter Richards

VERSE PRESS
Amherst, MA

ZEPHYR PRESS
Brookline, MA

Published by Verse Press and Zephyr Press

Library of Congress Cataloging-in-Publication Data

Richards, Peter, 1967-
  Nude siren : poems / Peter Richards.-- 1st ed.
      p. cm.
  ISBN 0-939010-74-7 (alk. paper)
  I. Title.
  PS3568.I31665 N83 2003
  811'.6--dc21

                                          2002012963

Available to the trade as a Zephyr Press title through
Consortium Book Sales & Distribution, 1045 Westgate Drive,
Saint Paul, MN 55114.

Cover image:
Turtle, 1993
SX-70 Polaroid photograph
Morgan Cohen
Image appears courtesy of the artist and Gallery NAGA,
Boston, Massachusetts

Book designed and composed by J. Johnson.
Text and Display set in Adobe Caslon.

Printed in Canada

9 8 7 6 5 4 3 2 1

First Edition

MASSACHUSETTS CULTURAL COUNCIL

for Tanya

Acknowledgments

Both: "Reading Oui"

Bridge: "Edict," "Thursday with Shawl," "Waiting for You"

Colorado Review: "Dear Mecca," "The Same," "For Me the Appearance," "The Lord Is My Portion"

Conduit: "Beige," "Eater"

Days of Poetry and Wine (Slovenia): "Nude Siren"

Electronic Poetry Review: "Plaza," "Red Boy, Red Girl," "Sandpiper with Roofer," "The Glass Tree"

Euphony: "Mallows," "The Contiguous Woman and the Contiguous Man, Together at Last"

Fence: "Lycidas," "Sleeper Car"

Harvard Review: "Nude Siren," "Sullen Girl with Branch Speaking"

Jubilat: "The Fighting Spiders of Bogeo"

Kontur (Croatia): "Coastal People"

Nerve: "Reservoir"

Optimus Prime: "Composition," "The Note"

Ploughshares: "Aster," "Dear Rome," "The Idea for Skate Mouth"

Verse: "Dear Jerusalem," "In the middle ear of man," "The Physical"

I wish to thank Barbara Richards and John Richards for their ongoing love and support. Thanks to Brian, Matthew, Cris, Jay, and Lori for their stewardship. Special thanks to Tomaz and Tanya for their insight and guidance.

CONTENTS

Nude Siren 11

Coastal People 12

Manteau 13

Red Boy, Red Girl 14

The Idea for Skate Mouth 15

The Lord Is My Portion 16

The Physical 17

Is There a Booth 18

Crayon 19

Beige 20

Lycidas 21

The appetite of this bored red cushion 22

Eater 23

The Fighting Spiders of Bogeo 24

Dear Jerusalem 26

Doth 27

For Me the Appearance 28

Days Of 29

Sandpiper with Roofer 30

Sleeper Car 31

Manchester Star 32

Hazen 33

Poem 34

The Glass Tree 35

Thursday with Shawl 36

Edict 37

At the fair the solemnity of her dress 38

Burial Sand 39

Setting 40

Sitting with Asa 41

Lake Tear of the Clouds 42

The Same 43

Picture Night Picture   44
Gusset   45
Dear Rome   46
The Sun   47
Kissing Asa   48
State Park   49
English Blood   50
The Bulb of Percussion   51
The Orange Cloud   52
Reading Oui   53
Lead Sheet   54
The Bulb of Percussion   55
Fortune   56
The Resort   57
In the middle ear of man   58
Composition   59
From the Afternoon   60
Approach   61
Esperanto   62
Dear Mecca   63
Mallows   64
The Bulb of Percussion   65
Sullen Girl with Branch Speaking   66
Plaza   67
Aster   68
The Contiguous Woman and the Contiguous Man,
        Together at Last   69
Death   70
Philter   71
Waiting for You   72
Reservoir   73
Being Late   74
Away from you the seafloor's longitudinal   75
The Note   76
Dear   77

Nude Siren

There is a nude siren in the jelly.
She cannot sing, she is dissolving.
During plantation song
she never struck me in secret.
She did strike me in the Patio of Oranges
as an anxious colonnade soldier
half way touching the assembled.
The new balcony powder falls to her eyelids.
Let her hind legs be accepted.
They lived here.
They raised good hind leg children
and leave the earth pilfering
only small handfuls of math.
They do not perceive death as vehicular
but rely on soft lickings to transfer
one life onto another.
There is a nude siren in the jelly.
She cannot sing, she is dissolving.
Her nakedness has no place in my poem.
Her breasts appear generally happy.
They seem full of self-awareness
and unafraid of the note I place between them.

Coastal People

Easter's hatred forces my lavender hand.
It is not the underside pattern of ice
making coastal people rise up near the embarrassment level
where they deliberate whether to love me or not.
Nor is it that point where they link listening
to a seasonal mistress subdivided by men.
What a pleasure to purposely set down a plate
and not to have asked.
Coastal people are always the first to forgive me.
They all saddle up to me, even the half-breeds saddle up to me.
In their paradise disagreements have risen.
Some would define me as a June-fed incinerator
where the virgins of Montreal lay glassed-in,
spat upon, and barking out questions construed as a dance.
I bite my thumb at these insipid little pricks.
They'd sell you a garland of dry rivers if given the chance.
There is one among you who conceals a lavender
dial at the flesh side of your hair. You practice
conception by raking foam rivulets into a briar.
God how I love it when the questioner strikes me —
where are you?
at the dial unbranching my best people.
I walk these hills wearing an Easter dress.
Cover your mouth when you see me
and the oven's black hay twines into a grid.

Manteau

Every day the world reassembles like a paw
from the coughed-up kestrel world. It wants
to be coughing up corn without patience
and Jacob's little tit mouse licking products
with an oily finish. The day enjoys sweets
but only when they press up against me.

Together we lie in the lawns of retardation.
We pick at the lawns like kestrel picking
her paw out from the little outsets
kestrel gave me this fondness for time
hissing in the holes of the paw. Time,
like a very large scallop writhing beneath me.

Kestrel, let the world be gone with you
for you are that blood splattered fink.
You cannot control the annals by which
corn regards me, nor will I wince during
visible head. Sweets, please enroll me —
I have the word aux inscribed on my skull
and it feels like I pee the patriotics of sleep.

Red Boy, Red Girl

Red boy, red girl, where do you often go sailing.
Where do you under small sailboat auspices
hear the hiss of a fruit informing its sections.
In the very last province I saw you kicking
my tiny and lockable head. One fresh
hemisphere splits to reveal me informing
on both of my sections: red boy, red girl,
fruit is a butcher where deep in the afterlife
Joshua can see you peeling Wheelwright
down to his sections. In afterlife there is more
than one woman and I can feed on them both
like an abyssinian cat licking his pill free of pâté.
I'd lick with my finger the cob of their approval
but why are you crushing my head
down to its lender, down to its very last gland,
and I am that reproachful vascular dollop.
Red boy, red girl, I'm afraid to let you strike me
even a little. Such welts leave a dinginess
that cause me to shout O invincible sick river
wearing medieval pants . . . Red boy, red girl,
at the first boot-heel to my head I remember only
being happy. I remember some very clear sediment
that grew in a fable. Themeless and without moral,
it feels like a grain being licked from the inside.

The Idea for Skate Mouth

The idea for moth came when soliciting the moth.
Moth? is there more than one solitary powder?

Moth: CONTIGUOUS END-TIME PELLETS
PRECEDE THE GRACKLE SUPPER RING.

The idea for elk came when I felt this elk was rejecting me.
I looked at him and he looked at me but the sensation was missing.

It was as if I had finally found the forest's true pantomime
and the voluminous braid to his glad sorrel heart.

When the elk twitches I want nothing from men.
When he runs off I see these tiny idiotic cathedrals inflecting the past.

The idea for skate mouth came when I was fishing for blues
off Cape Hatteras. It was nighttime and it felt like a dare.

Without a friend, survey, or trace of red weather,
I crept over the worlds and fingered the vent.

The Lord Is My Portion

With respect to size the forecaster piles on
the different sizes. No matter the volume
the forecaster tries to make them fit.
Notwithstanding constricts to a bus trip
unspeakable — one untaken seat
forcing an amulet too large to fit inside me.
Some foreign letters rub off a little
and a fragrance forms just to be near me.
Forecaster, make me cry.
I despise everything gilded and disobey
the kingfisher's destroyer code.
I allow only six forecasters a year
to explore my different sizes. Six is not
the enemy of my resting place, nor upon
a consul do the eyes of six remain — what?
kindness pleaded? sanction deferred? No,
mankind camp songs box out the plovers
that caused me to cry. Make me cry.
I did the reunion girls before you could
have them and I suppose hatred works
beautifully if you already fear disrobing
my six different sizes. Make me cry.
I have taken the enemy out with a kiss
and together we are trying to make a home
where the kingfisher decoy stands by itself
gilded in peace.

The Physical

You have too many animals pausing inside you.
One twitch and the others pause to listen.
Look how they feed upon each other.
We call this breeding the burials.
Your tongue is coated with animals.
Your pulse is powdery,
your affect, orange and mongrel.
In daylight we infect each other.
At first you'll get this over-rehearsed-
flower-winding-over-a-stake feeling.
It opens for the animals pausing inside you.
And then you'll get this beige light
heaving a diffuse noon on the floor.
Barely a sun, the kind you can stare at
blunted by cloud.

Is There a Booth

sometimes you say skimming the pollen with your finger
the way nightfall her own lace tumbles out from a cleft
the day clenching just to make it hurt you say I so badly
needed these goblets thrust upon a season of badness
the season reclusive after losing a child
my last brooms fanning out into rain and of this evening's
interrogation which touch prevails over the winds
and the one death swollen wind
sang of dent-work on signs admonishing light not to think a little
not to think twice like the waiter who covets your body
whose most earnest declaration they lost in the mail
all he knows are rooftops from far up dilate into heat
that terraces vouchsafe pinkness
and when you say it all the parceled out wicks for a day
unbraid like a braid played backwards in time

Crayon

Length of my day drew a flag
there on the downward hill.
A red trumpet sank into grass

and I could not wait to be taken.
I stood in between two crenels,
a black ivy cloud incising the sun.

In the distance I could hear
a rippling flute and a helmet
with his breath rushing through.

Beige

On the body very new towels
leave little colored threads.
I would like to connect them
with all the rooftop balconies.
Though we all keep a secret beige
thread in place of the body,
in beige none of us knows
the other exists. To suggest
we are all just strands braided together
is to risk treason against the climbing flower.
O climbing flower . . . I can hear you
breathing low in the satellites.
Low in the satellites hangs a beige
thread passed over as mine. I once
knew a beige pug and though she ran
with a pack of pugs the impression
was different — in her ink well eyes
I could sink to an unknown depth.
When she snorted all the world
snorted with her. Years ago
she was kicked dead by a horse.

Lycidas

In the over sold height of its power
the fucked-up summer is dead.
The dead fucked-up summer,
the blank stare from the mound.
Like one of its eyes white-lidded.
One of its eyes where the slightest
participant burns the original
white thorn of a trumpet.

Like the sleep was remorseless and white.
Sleep's promontory glistens the foil.
Girls who read Virginia Woolf glisten
the most (though we do not read together
I know they glisten — at first ambient white,
then toe-pink and violet, colluding in stripes,
pin stripes glistening up and down their haunches).

Like a summer all evening long
the bass player fell from her skateboard.
There is no bass player but she appears
to take some berries again. If a leaf
shatters it's because she compelled it.
She made the red hills stretch in the sunset.
She made the floor virgin-wise and mean.
Because of her I say the word thou.

The appetite of this bored red cushion

The appetite of this bored red cushion
seems unassailable and proper hearing
your pollinated feet not exactly
rushing towards me I can hear red
thinking why should I endure this life
in the corner and who else gets chosen
for knowing the full veldt of your weight
my prayer for you to sit beside me
has this new antelope fawn limping inside
and it often but never fatigues
surveying a long necklace of diminishing
waterholes where a red cushion floats
on the water always but never lapping
the water.

Eater

Possibly the fruits of comparison will not change
your daughter from churning her insides into a world.
At the very outer world a chained horse speaks in my sleep.
They both lie chained beneath me and in this landscape
neutral colors assign the word taproot onto a spring.
In the morning I taste the both in one of them
as a terrible midsection uncovering something to do.
But the one dried horse sticks like a wafer onto my tongue.
One morning I saw this flattened dry horse kicking a mother.
I saw my own mother brushing a new horse into a laugh.
The comparison sat alone to itself, her companion too.
Sometimes when I look in the paper there is the actual paper.
It records how a gray palm circles the wagon. Mother,
I fear you are indifferent to the foxgloves within me.
I fear my corrections are destructive and to speak
of one's mother is a kind of villainous maintaining of birth.
Still I'm one of those people who really dig food
arriving in spoonfuls that cause me to choke.
I say to myself — Eater, all you have is this body to bury
and the true miracle is if you don't somebody will.

The Fighting Spiders of Bogeo

There is that glass hull of sated people
who traffic in cardinal death.
Death always saying you've made
cardinals of us all, even though we have not.

In death the sod walls of Vinland
stand before me sixty head thick
and to the North free of contagion.
An orb weaver can pass through

quicker than thinking.
She has august-thin legs
and a head that is truly human-facial.
An orb weaver can pass through

only when eating cardinal brain.
Quick little vents appear
in between cardinals, suggesting
if worship alone could force stem folds

to go meiotic, still I would not worship.
If one could learn to palpate her dove-gray
colander pulses, still I would not palpate.
The ray spider speaks softly at first —

neutral sentiments designed to calm:
WE ARE AS ONE FROM THE SEASON NO SPIDER SHOULD ASK THIS.
In the evening she becomes more intimate:
TO ME YOUR EYES ARE AS IMMUTABLE

AS TWO CRUSHED SPIDERS RESURRECTED FOR VENGEANCE.
Eventually she just bites you
and after days of drinking your sleep
retires to her own little nook in the vestment

visually recalling three or four things.

Dear Jerusalem

The anti-Christ will carry
an auburn baggy. He seeks
to deceive no one and broods
like a barrier reef.

More gentle than his prequel,
he wants us to have habitual sex.
He has his gray hand towels
of parental sadness.

He has his sofa derived from gists.
Antlers diffuse and sprinkled
throughout the menu, he has
his sliding scale for judging

odalisques (it butters with thunder,
butters better than thunder).
I see a lather of kites lifting the lamb.
I see Matthew amplified into long stones.

I want there to be the record of smells.
I want yours to be pickled and mine
to be boiled. The slightest hint
of labellum fills me with cream.

I once slept with an injured stewardess.
Her name was Melissa
and she had more freckles.

Doth

I was trying to keep my primrose from sweating,
when a chained dancer whispered the word doth.
Mere doth, with its one size investigation of doth,
solicits gowns of nightly fabled doth.
Mere doth, where the dispatching tenors
brought doth to agree — no doth should hide
from its terrestrial nature, nor omit the first
defects of doth. In Cyprus the candles are hiding —
audience to the blinding indifference of doth.
In Sacramento the dancers are free and doth discuss
the verities of doth. One doth whispers to another —
"Doth? Are you there Doth? Doth are you there?"

For Me the Appearance

For me the appearance had nothing to do with us.
For me I prefer the pink to be lifted.
For me it seems the spirit finally interpolates.
For me she was lingering by choice.
There are those recanting tunnels.
It is like I have found someone very precious.
For me the candle eats.
For me some of you really are mother fuckers.
The four bodily humors now venture beyond a farce.
The visible flint sparks.
The sooner we trade hands.
For me I just like to comb other people.
For me exist the two melons: now and then.
A little hydrocortisone.
I hear puma sounds at certain heights.
For me Christ was quicker.
There is an actual smith, he pulses cloudwork over the land.
The visible ray flower.
For me father lay the partridge down and looked upon it.
For me to have otherwise suggested.
For me to position the colonel.
Not to lay still.
I could hear the boys in the boathouse cursing.
For me the aphid.
For me we have this past tension.
The whole outer circle but somebody spoke.

Days Of

I walk away from the past
holding my swan shaped companion.
Of small tendency the hairs of his beard
seem unreasonably wet. They scuffle
with one another like deceased and laughable
figures spied from the inside of a deposition
where the food is ornamental, the décor
immodest and base. I want to say one
among you is a blond athletic soothsayer
who delivers me with long summertime kisses
but then (self-consciously) the past brings
a napkin to her chin and I can see going
home with the coatroom, adjusting the hairs.

Sandpiper with Roofer

The marrow I suck from a sandpiper's leg
tastes like a laundered pez only half as sweet.
I guess part of me expects to begin walking
that way, while another part speaks freely
with critters the sandpiper ate. Critters
from the sea notoriously leave my body
in slightly pondered shapes. Sandpiper,
be happy you don't have to rip shingles
from a rooftop and blaze that way in the sun.
Rooftop, what are you most anxious about?
That this boy with jagged hair will not slip
and hang for a long time — shirtless, sweating,
and gripping your edge? Compared to nineteen
autumn passes I consider him to be more beautiful.
The double-sided sea on his shoulder.
The background wilderness telling him my mouth
is a chalice. I can see him pounding my face.
I can also see aging happily with nothing but that.
Sandpiper, let this be the last time you disparage
my leisure — my cat is only eleven months old
and already he's nonchalant about his vertical leap.
He sits on my bookshelf like a cross-eyed upuaut.
All morning he goes from room to room searching
for you. We both agree you should take your leftover
spirit and recede once and for all into the foam.

Sleeper Car

Black as a circle and with the arched foot of the futurist,
Anna grows older marching into my back.
Wincing unquietly allows me the first ever clearing
where our two ages rub like a locomotive. I enjoy
almost losing a hand skimming the walls of the tunnel.
The hurt part is flavor and like a whistle's bent wheel
names for the cities unstrangle together.
When do the cities stop touching? What is my attribute?
"Wave to the hill," whispers Anna.
"Wave to the hill," whispers everyone.
Her orange corset of sequins was something I did.
"Crouch with your teeth," whispers Anna.
"Crouch with your teeth," whispers everyone.

Manchester Star

Today I was given notice: the three circling
seasons have uninvited me to their pool.
Voicelessly swimming there, I was often called
the scaly one. Little help shouting, No one
can love or be loved without first touching
my body. Now at night when I sit in my Celica
I recall just how pleasant it was to be among them.
Such odd swimmers, debating whether to touch me
or not. I remember one season absentmindedly
grilling an orange. I remember the dog shit
caught in the tread of her sandal. O how she
passively watched me work it out with a key.
Yesterday she ushered me into her recess room.
She asked if I would circle three times around her.
She asked if I would trace true cross-hairs just beneath
her shoulder. And what it must feel like to live
without ever once overlapping a season.
I answered awkwardly, disembodied, mistrustful,
even though I wasn't. So what if I'm the scaly one.
Last night when I saw her lethargically patting
the end of the pool, I knew in my heart of hearts
swimming among them made me a season.

Hazen

I need to realize I'm one of those girls things happen to. Last week was almost a witness box in itself. I got to the place not believing our lips had actually touched, but she stranded the evening in Pennsylvania and we had quite a conversation looking at snow from our separate windows. We agreed we had both been deceived and parted our legs without imagination. Brightness in the room left me blowing sometimes on her hand. I saw each finger working its own trade and how sometimes the great dangers I see can lend a little help. They say a woman, the third time sinks into goodness, but she is not like other women. This I heard from the snow after I hung up the phone. The next night found itself embraced in a car we had somehow gotten hold of. Her mouth a cloudless half-day and for about a mile burning my hand. Little red-coats bayed in the mist and with their countermarch resting I found new scabbards burning the heather. What heather? Well, I can tell you I crouched inside for a long time sucking her off like an oath. The breath in her sleep is quiet — there is no sound of any hurt. Listening to her breathe I was no longer afraid hearing news from those I had lost.

Poem

I have taken your trumpet into a bad sheet
of paper where it does not circular breathe
a vigilant girl kicking my face is a habit
acquired while risking subhuman forms.

To say she was kicking the courier
is to pack each vista into an oven
where this tall savant that I love
spoke briefly of hurt.

Elbow colors, daylight colors,
colors by their own free will
return to the bed where I lived
as a benign hook maneuvering heat

down through the question
should it even persist. Well then,
a great gale washing my hair feels
like your waistcoat's murmuring voice.

It leaves nothing like an odalisque smell
or the dead congealing as a really good plan
they had no time to make.

The Glass Tree

The glass tree left behind by a blossoming
tree waits in the debitage of its untaken
filament. Sulking, for other trees left behind
blossoming kingdom trees where some
nevertheless chromatic evil takes away moisture
until the subject is puma polishing the sign
for clear. O feline contamination forever
lounging in the poem where I relinquish
a tree which is the sainthood of a very tall
fang reflecting my glass-based alternate
system for tree. At dusk I need to devour
newborns I gave to myself. No, I need to rest
here, upon this glass limb, the flick of my tail
conducting my rest.

Thursday with Shawl

This new glove trying her honest best.
And this glove stuck to the tongs
held for dipping frightened hair.
Rinsing at home I did not seek
permission, nor did I serve sincerely
those recruits they asked me to serve.
Hairs skid on the water.
At the very top of the water hairs skid
and not just because since was the word
disguising a bet. Walking home
I can hear home wanting the back room
papered in gloves. I can hear home
washing my body — translucent,
but not really, like a fountain sharing
the milk, or a white dune enjoying
my pupil. My problem is a clear glove
once fixed to the wall turns opaque.
I can't decide if the wall is surfacing
or if the words once used for home
frighten each other, holding hands?

Edict

To carry on first depilate my body
from either a frictionless or solid position.
From a body renowned with bad overlapping
eggs, a little 14th century anterior naturally
ejects. Disregard as you would the clear
plasma on a motherboard pawned hastily
by a nurse conditioned to field sorrow
from a predatory and now less fed-upon state.
Her name is not Grenadine and though she was
bred to carry the words human-hat power
to the increased and lindrical edge, my own
face resembles that powdery elbow where time
conditions a face to atone once and for Grenadine
the undone circuits of my possible face.
I have noticed living away from each other
tends to encourage dreams of human-hat power.
Plums, bilges, wreaths, intrigues, and the whole
host of spiritual foam left me feeling badly
exposed in the damp glens of helmet ennui.
I know that my deeds (whether good or decided)
can never be enshrined by a new hat's greater hold.
I also know it was not until the human-hat reformers
began the practice of publicly undressing Grenadine
that my own arm was called upon to punish my face.
What my elbow had done for Germany and France,
the human-hat reformers did to my crown.
From hereon hat wearing is enrolled in this book
and I call upon all good subjects to war against it.

At the fair the solemnity of her dress

At the fair the solemnity of her dress
became my inability to manage the past.
People were sharing food beneath a tent.
The locket she wore did not swing open
or begin marking time from breast to breast.
From this green tiled room one of my fears
alights on the crushed grass again.
In death that fear is my owner, but here,
right now, recalling the fairgrounds,
I can lie on this slab purposeless and free.
Wind is a broken off piece of the fair.
Should I appear as a living person
I will ask her to know me.

Burial Sand

Perfume from your spectrum heats me from below.
Both rise as a question: what have you done
to my population? Transition hens. Police
who feed on the glacier before I was born.
No, they eat spectrum. Spectrum and only
spectrum delivers your ass to my hand
like a suitcase unattended in a mosque.
Tiny violet black iris mouth. Chest
anger for eyes. Lips breaded with thistle.
How does it feel to be living in the forest
of rook skin? forest skin? skin skin?
skin of the unrealized ballerina?
So many noontime gospels of hair.
Ointment from the blue end always
first to evaporate. Ointment and always
these difficult red shifts found me
a house I could not own.

Setting

Sun with its loose towel
loves me like a sister.
Lets me in the evening
longer than I should.

At the small of her back
will she leave me?
From the small of her back
where will I go?

Sitting with Asa

Sitting with Asa I can foresee
a porridge like hell breaking
through to the surface.
A little bit floats up like a bay leaf
in the pacific. At the smote
castratos are cruising
and I awaken to bay leaves
strapped to my feet. Overseeing
the wake a bay leaf is brittle
and can shatter if played with.
If skipping porridge constitutes
play, only the bay leaf can know.
I do know steam brings pliancy
to a bay causing a leaf less likely
to break. And for some days
Asa won't even eat. Together
we sit enjoying the wait.

Lake Tear of the Clouds

Add to it smells of yonder painting
her nails in a devastated chair
and I can feel swaddled here watching
your indifferent waist move to the sect
my address prepared for you. The same
aloof handbag sunning on a boulder.
Same feeding mantis completing
touches of light across your hair —
a late Syracuse birthplace where the entire
headdress seemed surprised. Marcy,
the day will come when ethnicity is a clear
rose particulate floating above my person.
My person, like a huge alpine clover
with quick cushioning sighs.

The Same

The same appears in a basement
where the free standing apparel
made the next day impassively quiet.

Beforehand the same whispers
"I should warn you, I'm a real shaver."

The same invites me to pose for the evening.
I lay with my hip between two warring horses.

In the painting the light is diffuse
suggesting a false dedication.
If only my anklet counted for something.
If only the sash undone in the end.

In the painting I stare with a spoiled afghan look about me.
The spoon appears to be inwardly setting.
The white bowl sloughing its parallel rooms.

Picture Night Picture

I am that tiny animal who eats the whistle
from your gland. For too long now
my mouth hosted these big baroque ideas
so that I could kneel there in the masticatory
shade of my own threshing — sensing too much,
too little, even one unrehearsed groan leaves me
sipping motherless streams directly from your hand.
My mouth is not a mouth but condensed by serene
aerial slaves who converge directly on a vessel —
tissue from your changing mind.
Tissue from your changing mind plays an impatient
role regulating the disputed forms of nuance, exertion,
and musical fears. It seems to me the softer the whistle,
the louder the fear, and now I expire deep in that pouch
suspended between your adjacent deviations:
the spray orchestral, the aftertaste sad.

Gusset

Your hip bone of unreserved court time
heaving a plaid sail over the land.
All morning do I need to tell you
I saw a dead baby pilot openly staring from inside a wave.

It felt like he was angry with me for being that way.
Like he thinks I walk around thinking

time being the lowest form
of down in the dunes overcooked semen.
Christ slept apart from the others.
Light, hand me a pen named Sara.

It began as a prodigal cloud
heating three different rooms
and two barbarian children
sadly wearing your skirt.

I say sadly like sadly the armrest is changing
with a lie it decides to have told.

Dear Rome

Sometimes I touch the cleaner.
Sometimes an hourly vole
shares the bed and wife with me.
Once I sat up suddenly and spoke it:
crowned platelets inherit the passenger bin.
I believe the precise moment of Rapture
is felt not to occur, the Rind of Incidence
I made up in the first place.
On a clear day the majority of Ice Age
mammals give me serious wood.
Where I sit the Eucharist passes beneath me.
It barely fits, but it fits,
like the pattern of new behemoths
hoisting aqua parasols, but with indifference.
They march to avoid the two Ann Margarets
showering together in a prison way before
Midnight Express even came out.
When they embrace cross-legged
it's like a red and sun-lit wooly latch.
They can hum all they want
but when their tusks begin touching
I get this strong solarium smell
thinking up poetry for the external world.

The Sun

With her long view of Pittsfield
the sun never learned to read
and wears a pendant to remember
the luxury of soil doubling its own
amarcord trait for she is a variation
on soil selected from a hedgerow
of changing friendships and color
the words exertion and mascara
really do lie down together trading
troublesome coins or just some
mouth to mouth from time to time
the sun's rays say to me trebuchet
of the mind grazing pendent
when I finally do open parasols
regard themselves as accidental milk
arriving inside these little sevilles
a found head some of us hid
some of us are hiding hailstorms
inside a piper my own sediment
where the bugles of no rage
are also pumping colors.

Kissing Asa

Kissing Asa time has removed
the midsummer tires. Where
they have gone to is better off
withstanding the dead.
As far as I'm concerned
the dead can dismember a sequin
for as long as they do.
The dead tear with their teeth,
tear with their guile, they can even
tear with a plum.
Though I would not let them
mess with our kissing,
one kiss floats to the surface
on a green and barnacled plum.

State Park

No one should piss this freely,
but I do. O bunting egg.
O Lord. Thank you for keeping
the grasses evil and smooth.
The park ranger is female.
She wears a stiff green ranger outfit
over her leotard of soft yeti hair.
She gave me a formal warning.
She gave me Bob Kaufman by the fire.
In twilight tasks proceeding new arrivals,
she gave me this site dilated by force.
A site thinking for itself, all by itself.
O deep in the hurry penultimate screw.

English Blood

As a rule the English travel in highly
unlikely circles where the concept
of repair is a cat licking its prick.

I know this English couple when they speak
of their energy a red and shiny one
uncoils serenely overhead.

How should I describe an Englishmen
when he stands closer than expected?

How should I account for my own English blood
when thanksgiving with mom and dad
sends either a corkscrew into the future,
or a corkscrew into the past.

I'm not saying the English will eat their own
if given the chance, but faced with a little frost
eating their own is exactly what they do.

The Bulb of Percussion

on the outside the past is a good public skater
with long unintended hair beneath the doorway
of a steamer she plays a game of decoration
the card in her hair faceless and with the pretense
of a queen giving off some good immigration odor
porters below stammer sincere leader light is done
light ambles into my lap where the nude sits
bisected by lulls and becoming a real showoff
busier and busier until the very last doorway is sea
the sea with its blue aging crayon
the crayon because actually this is our fault
and it feels like those are some waves
like these are the waves all life is like
and we should not chronicle kiss in a language
where the names agree we do not exist

The Orange Cloud

The orange cloud
twitches to a blue fin,
spines in the fin,
concussion of foil.

An infant's pinto fish
gnaws serenely on the water.

Some incise the water
with pink Tahoma's capital n —
an everlasting bromide of love.

Thistle let out by a traitor.

Some fleabane prosperity.
Some pig nose guitar.

Reading Oui

That woman's ear is a geode quarry in early summer.
The word geode backlit perfectly by professional
sound and light people. Between sets women
from the Ponds Institute whisper to each other:

Yolanda, the fact of your stamina is a guest wind
only a mother can know. This time try it without
deliberately hatching a pause. No, I want you to gasp
less as a monument and more like a skiff.

God bless the occasional terry-cloth head-band.
God bless the one subject upon which two car washers agree:
in the days of our own harlequin mist
we are links in a net seining forevers.

A worm's ear is said to hover.
That woman's ear seems lower than the other.
It seems serenely confected. In sunlight it holds
a red branch of soundless water.

Lead Sheet

I see a lead sheet standing all by itself.
The darkness inside barely twitches
so that finite cinemas of snow
rise up sporadically, then trail off
leaving these black muted iris sores.
I unwrap myself saying snow
where can I pat you
without crushing a starling?
One month to a lead sheet is a month to us all.
It is walking all by itself and with a mixture
of green light wetting the hair.
Walking towards those who are mowers,
it brings sudden changes to hair
and an ice probe not reaching the end of its cord.

The Bulb of Percussion

The past sits inside and ponders her love.
She brushes her hair, black and translucent
down to her nipple. Of the few tones
together the two of us make, one partially
decides not to be so latent. Vengeful
enough my organs seem easily averted.
They wait floating in pans where the past
watches me wait. In pans my intestine
reflects so easily. What else? I guess
I'm afraid to let light smudge even a little.
The rest of me sticks to the business side of the pan.
Now I can see I was always partly in love.
As if to say "Lord, here is your napkin,"
my body assumes a pink and white foam.

Fortune

I sleep in the bee's mouth.
It feels my parents are far away.
It feels full of color,
crowded — a sadness
that does not surround me.

Last night my friend
awkwardly spoke of his clown.
I could not see him.
What will happen to the shears
held close to my body?

Body, I am so angry with you.
My descriptions of your mouth
are uneven. They wear loose
fitting shorts that hide
the gulf-stream bays of your power.

In vain the mascara I lifted from Osco.
In vain drafting by hand
new objects conceived by pneumatic men.
They lick the smear in my palm
from crushed glittery pellets.

In the morgue we look at my hair.
Leaning over we see my own face
reflected all day in the pool
where the spike went through.
In vain tongues that polish a hand.

The Resort

By midmorning the girls of Lordosis
try on new tops all around the pool.
With jade speed regattas of swan
pass between their scissoring kicks.
In death I was sometimes a bather,
sometimes a swan, and the intervals
trailing between left pink little plumes
behind bathers searching for air.
But a swan is more than one
and ejects blood upon the bathers.
With bathing not everyone awakens
to find their workstations buried in hair.
To their kiosk vetted like an actual hood.
Widowed without ever holding tresses.

In the middle ear of man

In the middle ear of man
there is a chain of three bones.
Tonight women in unison call it the anvil cloud.
I would like for us all to live independently
on the carpet — thunderheads in argot
dissolving our sexes. Do you remember
the girl on the mud flap? A likeness,
she keeps me well hidden. If sand lilies
climb the base of my horn, the Pauline
Letters bleed onto her thigh. I carry
a clear and purely symbolic blue liquid.
I carry an involuntary surface
coinciding with sea level.
Once, when cornered by spotlight,
I bandied my pasties for all the prom to see.

Composition

Try not to think of past participles
as scar tissue divided evenly
amongst the masses. Time may
change the way you think of men
(change, say the way teeth marks
fade into a gull) but like a brook
left out in the open its intentions
are guarded. In the future perfect
our near miss of mothers
heckle the wind. They water-log
together in vast obligatory clouds.
They know when to lie sanguine into a ditch.
Sanguine has no use for us — she
is above us in quiet, above us in death,
and the high plains blister her sleep.
The mornings toweling off
fill me with inner suggestions.
They suggest to themselves and to me
who cannot hear the morning.

From the Afternoon

Autumn has gone
and left you her feather
gray boa dusting
trophies in their case.

Resplendent forehands
never came through
and you follow them
all the way to forgetfulness.

Who can hear heads
of the strawflower
dropping off, ricochet,
orbiting flats of alyssum —

dead, unplanted, drying as hair.

Approach

For you I keep contours, they clatter discreetly.
I open like that and with the slender unvanquished legs.
Please touch me with the long frond of the future.
Please, as with Heathrow appearing in haste.
When we touch I frighten but I do not contract
like a spoiler. A newly tightened and outdated spoiler
and with the blond neck hair of sun-lacquered haze.
My outer leg lay bitten by flies. When they alight I can hear
the manufactured voices — genesis can save you
but only as a child. When your companion left
for the station he did not turn you over or ask you
to carry his books. To forego salad is hiding.
Deep in the outtakes Calypso lay rearranging herself.
Pollen on the water may have consulted but now she's
breathing a neither. In the bunk beds you can hear it.
In each bunk bed ever slept in you can hear it —
Calypso's diffident breathing spied upon by fawns.

Esperanto

You are that cup for the truly colored.
That hand from the commune buried in haste.
A commune raising flame-retardant heather
and their new flag of indigenous hurt
signals to me poor Sahara abbreviation,
living this way will not give you suffrage.
My desire for a gold experience presses
discomfort into the crease. I like to watch you
vacillate (tending largesse) for you are that
dame with culprits paving her skirt.
As though all my lives fill up
with wonderful ones, you are sand boxes
and retaining walls of little cheer.
As though without anger you seem so far
above. You have tattoos of cauliflower
consuming your hand. Your hand not buried
giving a seer from Georgia conflicted sleep.
Sleep of the savior, sleep of the hunt. Sleep
saying poor Sahara abbreviation, I meant to end
each morning exactly as you but then I cannot.

Dear Mecca

Unbelievers remove the fruit stands.
They keep larches and master them.
In the snow with their snow bundles
they all hide themselves.

They lather your sister with law.
She lies down naked, without any clothing.
She makes great projections in the night.
She is wet with the rain of our children.

Alone, the law touching itself.
We love each other.
We laugh and argue in the market.
We often go and test walkie-talkies.

We never buy them.
We are naked, without any clothing.
I have a cyst that she worries about.
I keep a kind of freckle-chart

for the freckles on her back.
She has this marvelous peaceful ease.
In the park today sleeping
everyone could see her.

Mallows

The different sizes were inserted.
The different sizes with hidden
hind legs because the true hind leg
believer can never be outed.

Devotions — each one bred
to fit the different sizes,
wane vertically under a dome.

It's like that endless grid of haddock
seen just before sleep, or the future
theater of neo-placement, when
we all together play the same girl.

The Bulb of Percussion

The past sits inside washing her body.
So many torch lit rivulet sounds.
But the nightly voices,
in a moment's notice they can possess her.
Already I can hear in the future
when by accident her elbow gongs the tub again.
What future?
when together we cry into a sock.

Sullen Girl with Branch Speaking

Let's just say if July could wager
the erstwhile of heaven, her black
denim shorts wouldn't prevent it.
And that by her second day in America
she had already mastered a hog.
That the sheen from her clogs is less
than the saddened phases in a gouache,
in no way inhibits the gleam from her shoulder.
She did not lead me to a plaza.
We intoned nothing amongst ourselves.
Not to have touched her is to convulse like an omen.

Plaza

In the tawny rustic sun your gelato
looks wrinkled and devil-spit capable
whereas the cocoon of your crushed
cinnabar tube seems finely gauged
and crocheted to resist the wrestled
nozzle of my arid horn not holding
a spoon or adorned with multiplying
ethnographic designs whose numbers
are saying tonight's open ribbed yoke
would look so absolute juxtaposing
alternate panels on a whisper-sheer
oxblood skirt made for the fetching
georgette two of us both with a wide
smocked waistband and a verdigris
silk lining that actually breathes.

Aster

Among the peopled flowers my legitimate crankiness
forced into diasporas, none have been more far flung
than the aster. I do not understand how such star structures
are formed. Unlike me, the aster throws rays blazing
from white to pink or purple about a disk that is usually yellow.
Flower heads of a composite type leave me feeling resentful
of the morning. As with other flowers I hate how the aster
comes in a bunch-weight measured in grams. People do not
speak of this. Nor do they speak about the aster's advanced
spaceborne winter emissions. From the aster came
this school of film proclaiming the divinity of gas.
We are always just imagining instruments reflecting the earth.
The aster is a platform for announcing the interplay
between sun, grooming, and the girls who teach me sortilege.
With its rounded blunt edges of true speechlessness, the aster
(because of me) can no longer speak. We should
all undress obediently affecting the aster's oceanic regard.
From the aster came a very tall woman dismissing the Lord.
From the aster this tight little bell retracting the calm.

The Contiguous Woman and the Contiguous Man, Together at Last

He gave me a necklace of secret horse caves.

Each have their torch light of little golden fasteners
and bastard amber vaults of different fortress rhythm.

One flops to my chin like a jade pannier.

That I could rest there.

Death

You can keep your baton licked by pedestrians.
Keep corners where the oxbow of abundance
eats away at the boulevards where I often
do greet solicitors and hounds.
You can also just keep passing by for your voice
is a flicker sending little shout-outs to the past
where I never did confuse you as an ex-boyfriend
ex-girlfriend situation.
You are big and far and away the arbiter
dispensing seventy sheets of foil and I can smell
your nest is adorned with the burnt colors
of non-musical hair.
A basketry that will not regard me,
nor make a habit of me. Not me, who happily
did guide ponies of hairless chagrin. Not me,
sometimes sobbing into my pillow "the Green Line sucks."
Death, from your invisible place you want my humidity.
You have those odd-ball solar points and a breast plate
that romantically appeals to me. Still, dreading you
is good and passes through with little effect.
Death, for now you're just a phrase in my head
but when you do appear I promise to snap-to like a sail.

Philter

To make yourself beloved envision this large
and beautiful hand strumming the diamond
back girls who compose your congregation.
Feel that your most chief-eaten-dressed-as-a-puma
desire awakens to its own diamond interior.
Trust for yourself this hand and that juleps
concede the most inward path of the hand.
Grant fluid its own secret path, for even those
confederate vessels possess the cloud spouting
handles to prove it. Though faith for an ampulla
proves difficult to muster, let there be muster
and girls. The orange and feathery helmeted
girls carving the first new fiats of day.

Waiting for You

Endlessness has begun to bore
and makes partial claims at any rate.
Magnification suffers more
than if all the animals were tested.
Each segment an attempt to leave
the vigorous look of scenery
presupposing inert whereabouts
where a bradypod secretly mates
(modular feed announcing a lens
where the blood-mite prefers padded
lumps to ministered hair). As a physical
law Easter is a geometric organ where I
awaken to bailiffs crouching in the center.
I want to emphasize here that one man's
wife is another man's gull, that island
women have a way of saying I'm not really mean,
I'm not really mean, and this booth is enough
for an Anubis statue ingesting himself.

Reservoir

So what if you forgot your sister's slip
on a clear southern airfield. You can
still be this summer's wet nurse giving
up her first hysterical bedside marble.
Genuine scalp nervousness. Authentic
wet nurse outfit. O pregnant little fuck bird
where the two of us used to go swimming
and pretend it was the olden days —
your keyhole bandeau dries on a rock
and from now on none of us are stricken.
Tadpoles statuesque, specimen-free,
truly coded, embedded like twenty-two
chortles finally will swim. You allocate
beauty — the privilege to float in a stardom
pool where I can see your very first milk
feeding the numbers with number feed.

Being Late

Some eyeliner gives me a restful kiss
and some like your smell holding a glue gun
of rays to my head. During long red anteriors
of the first magnitude it's really not important
that your buckle resemble a sailfish breaching.
Though in that super gloom before we kissed
it did make quite a difference.

Away from you the seafloor's longitudinal

Away from you the seafloor's longitudinal
grasses pump their anxiety and New World
pretenses up past a thicket of foam where every
day the same gull sits taped to rock smoking
a Newport and waiting for his brother to deliver
the revised figures, the linoleum swatches.
Away from you the breezeway's hand-me-down
camisole sits attentively unfolding the stairs
where I saw you descend into the source of all waters,
a minnow of sunscreen alive in your hand.
What witness discourages my brain from unfolding
another gushing hyacinth whose tan lines lead
to a room already slandered, already recurring,
for the walls here are lathered with flowers,
flowers from the forties, absolutely hyacinths
repeating their death-gasp up past the ceiling
where some truly old money sits squirreled away
from one day installing a fan. If I were to shave you
and not avoid life. If I could just lie there beneath
you like a tidal pool utterly hopeless and open,
it would be as if I push upon a tube of cadmium,
the toxicity warning just now tarnishing off,
just now insinuated into the work, the lungs,
the blood, it's the blood where a word could not
keep itself still and falls away from the foil
and onto this paper I send along with a little
salt to the shiny red apex of you.

The Note

Out of the jelly my flying machine
swings part way over the balcony
where illness sits breathless and happy.
Behind each pillar illness sits drawing
her little drawings of overt applause.
Unavoidably at night my flying machine
appears as a village-like sky smelling
plainly of teardrops and afterbirth
highways where the fulcrum seems gentle
and no prophecy can stand assaulting
another. Watch out! for I do fly overhead
on my gingko tree motor and a gladness
that ruptures on behalf of that sponge
paying out vinegar into your hand.

Dear

I could you a crown of gray circulation flowers
and a dress printed with amulet corn
and a garland braided with unrestricted south-west saviors
(unobserved I can see them lovingly paint your brow)
and the undisciplined company of your hair
your hair's twilit austerity
your sleepy voice like a collapsing basket
and the counterpoise of perspiration reflecting the world
your clear pools of battlefield nectar
and that cheerful modest bulge from outer space
and this plan-absorbing footstool where you lean back like a trough
and all the pitiful meanwhiles
all the uncareful.

About the Author

Peter Richards was born in Urbana, Illinois. His previous collection *Oubliette* was published by Verse Press in 2001 and received a Massachusetts Center for the Book Honors Award. He teaches at Tufts University and lives in Somerville, Massachusetts.